CODE BREAKERS AND SPIES

Code Breakers and Spies of the Civil War

ANDREW CODDINGTON

Cavendish Square
New York

Published in 2019 by Cavendish Square Publishing, LLC
243 5th Avenue, Suite 136, New York, NY 10016

Library of Congress Cataloging-in-Publication Data

Names: Coddington, Andrew, author.
Title: Code breakers and spies of the Civil War / Andrew Coddington.
Description: New York : Cavendish Square, 2019. | Series: Code breakers and
spies | Includes bibliographical references and index. | Audience: Grades 7-12.
Identifiers: LCCN 2017050427 (print) | LCCN 2017051063
(ebook) | ISBN 9781502638472 (library bound) | ISBN
9781502638489 (pbk.) | ISBN 9781502638496 (ebook)
Subjects: LCSH: United States--History--Civil War, 1861-1865--Secret service--
| Juvenile literature. | Espionage--United States--History--19th century--Juvenile
literature. | Spies--United States--History--19th century--Juvenile literature.
Classification: LCC E608 (ebook) | LCC E608 .C63
2018 (print) | DDC 973.7/85--dc23
LC record available at https://lccn.loc.gov/2017050427

Editorial Director: David McNamara
Editor: Stacy Orlando
Copy Editor: Alex Tessman
Associate Art Director: Amy Greenan
Designer: Alan Sliwinski / Joe Parenteau
Production Coordinator: Karol Szymczuk
Photo Research: J8 Media

The photographs in this book are used by permission and through the courtesy of: Cover, p. 56 Buyenlarge/
Getty Images; p. 4, 20, 60 Bettmann/Getty Images; p. 12, 16 Interim Archives/Getty Images; p. 2,
38 Stock Montage/Getty Images; p. 28 North Wind Picture Archives; p. 31 Rose O'Neal Greenhow/
Peter Newark Military Pictures/Bridgeman Images; p. 34 Alexander Gardner/Library of Congress;
p. 36 GL Archive/Alamy Stock Photo; p. 41 Library of Congress/Wikimedia Commons/File:Signal
station Elk Mountain.jpg/Public Domain; p. 45 Niday Picture Library/Alamy Stock Photo; p. 51
RadioFan at English Wikipedia/Wikimedia Commons/File:Confederate cipher disk.png/CC BY SA
3.0; p. 58 Wikimedia Commons/File:Confederate 5 Dollars.jpg/Public Domain; p. 63 Fine Art Images/
Heritage Images/Getty Images; p. 65 U.S. Navy history website/Wikimedia Commons/File:Balloon
barge.jpg/Public Domain; p. 66 MPI/Getty Images; p. 68 Wavebreakmedia/Shutterstock.com.

Printed in the United States of America

Contents

CHAPTER 1

A NATION DIVIDED

I n the decades following its war for independence, the United States seemed to be a country on the rise. The government had effectively doubled the size of the nation through the purchase of the Louisiana Territory from France, securing access to the Mississippi River—a valuable trade route that promised to multiply America's economic output— as well as the Gulf Coast port of New Orleans, Louisiana. The explorers Meriwether Lewis and William Clark had charted much the lands to the west of the Mississippi all the way to the Pacific Ocean. Settlers migrated west, forming communities in places such as Texas, California, and Oregon. The war with Mexico that this wave of immigration had sparked was decided in the United States' favor in 1848.

That same year, an American prospector discovered a gold deposit outside San Francisco, California, igniting the country's first gold rush a year later and pulling billions of dollars from the ground. Less than a century after uniting under a common government, the United States seemed poised to stretch across the continent and take a place among the world's military and economic superpowers. Yet, despite everything that the young country had accomplished—and seemed destined to become—it all was primed to come crumbling down.

Spying in Early America

The typical image of the Civil War is neat ranks of blue-coated Union soldiers marching against gray Confederates, both sides squaring up to one another, taking aim with their rifles, and firing at each other. While it is true the Civil War's most famous battles played out according to this general formula, it fails to take into account one crucial aspect of war: espionage, or spying. Many of the Civil War's important moments took place on the battlefield, but the role of spying is often overlooked. Gathering military intelligence is an aspect of war that takes place in the shadows of night, the hush of forests, the quiet of private drawing rooms, the busy chatter of administrative offices, or the bustle of city streets.

Despite the crucial importance that spying had played in previous wars, it was almost completely neglected by both the Union and the Confederacy at the start of the war. Even so, both sides quickly realized the need for espionage and worked to build comprehensive intelligence networks. In the process, they developed technologies that would catapult them several years into the future and forever change America's relationship with spying.

Birth of American Espionage

In its infancy, America recognized the importance of military intelligence—in fact, it is possible that without a robust and reliable network of spies in its early years, the nation might not have even existed. During the Revolutionary War, George Washington made a point to cultivate military intelligence at every stage of the campaign. At the time of the Revolution, the British were widely considered to be the finest professional army in the world: troops were better equipped, divisions disciplined, officers well trained, and the army funded more than Washington's Continental Army could ever hope to be.

In order to tip the odds of winning the war in his favor, Washington would have to outsmart and outmaneuver his enemy, so he took what little resources he had and invested heavily in espionage and subterfuge. Faced with a superior enemy, Washington built what was arguably the most sophisticated and wide-ranging spy ring in the world at the time: the Culper Spy Ring, situated in New York City. Washington's informants included individuals from practically every walk of life in colonial America: sailors, business owners, artisans, and housewives, all of whom passed along intelligence about enemy troop sizes, movements, personal feuds between officers, and more.

These informants communicated in messages using codes. A code is a puzzle that protects the information

DID YOU KNOW?

As many as one hundred thousand Southern slaves escaped through the Underground Railroad between 1810 and 1850, according to the National Underground Railroad Freedom Center in Cincinnati, Ohio.

in a message by adding an additional layer of meaning that needs to be solved in order to reveal the original, true meaning. Done properly, a coded message would appear to anyone other than its intended recipient as gibberish.

In order to keep the codes straight, the Culper Spy Ring used a special code book that devised a special alphanumeric code for important key words, including places, names, and things. Coded messages are not always written down. In Washington's spy ring, for example, a woman named Anna Strong often communicated simple messages just by the arrangement of her laundry on the clothesline!

The Roots of Civil War

When the American colonies shrugged off British rule in 1776, they were presented with a complicated question: what sort of nation would they become? At the time, the colonies were a patchwork of different politics, economies, histories, and cultures. In general, the early states fell into one of two categories: the urban and industrialized Northern states and the rural and agricultural Southern ones. These distinctions coalesced into a single issue that would drive a wedge directly through the center of America: slavery.

The North and the South

Although slavery was common in both the North and South when the colonies were first founded, differences in climate and geography fundamentally changed the development of each region's economies and, as a result, their reliance on and attitudes toward slavery. The South's warm subtropical climate, fertile soil, and abundance of flat, sweeping fields supported the cultivation of "cash crops," valuable crops that are grown to be sold on the market rather than consumed by the grower. The wealthiest Southern farmers built sprawling plantations dedicated to the production of cash crops such as rice, corn, sugarcane, tobacco, and, most importantly, cotton.

In contrast, the Northern states tended to have colder climates and hillier, rockier land, which generally prevented the sort of large-scale agricultural production prevalent in the South. Instead, Northern economies focused on developing manufacturing and professional industries. By 1858, many Northern states had already abolished slavery, in part because of a growing religious movement that saw slavery as morally corrupt, but also because there really hadn't been a large need for slavery up until that point.

This focus on industry also meant that the North implemented and benefited from new technologies more than the South did. The North had better, more developed transportation and communication infrastructures, including 21,300 miles (34,279 kilometers) of railroad tracks and 45,000 miles (72,420 km) of telegraph lines. Together, this meant that the North controlled about 70 percent of the country's total rail and telegraph lines. The South, by comparison, had only 9,022 miles (14,519 km) of rail lines. Most of these led east–west, built to transport cash crops to shipping ports on the coast, and were traveled by older, slower, and less-efficient trains. Many engines were actually wood-fired, as opposed to coal-fired, requiring frequent stops for operators to cut lumber to keep the train moving.

The Southern plantation economy was the primary driver of slavery in the United States. In the years before the war, nearly four million black people were enslaved in the United States, and essentially all of them were located in the South. In 1860, there were forty-six thousand plantations throughout the South, each of which averaged fifty slaves, though the largest boasted several hundred. Plantation owners and other farmers relied on slave labor to perform backbreaking work. Because enslaved people were considered property, they worked without pay. They were often compelled to work by constant threat of violence by

Well before the Civil War broke out, a country-wide
clandestine operation had been working behind the
scenes to secretly ferry enslaved blacks in the South
to freedom: the Underground Railroad. The Railroad
was a loosely organized network of people throughout
the United States who helped runaway slaves along
certain paths north by offering food, supplies, money,
or homes and barns as places to rest.

The Underground Railroad got its name in
1831 after the new railroad lines that started
crisscrossing the country thanks to the new technology

This map shows many of the routes that conductors on the
Underground Railroad used to smuggle slaves to freedom.

of the coal-fired steam engine train, but its roots actually predate railroads by several decades. Evidence suggests that similar networks operated by the religious group known as the Quakers were in existence as far back as the eighteenth century. In 1786, George Washington complained that one of his slaves was assisted in his escape by just such a network.

Although the network of routes resembled that of rail lines, the name is misleading—the Underground Railroad was neither a railroad nor underground. It did take inspiration and code names from real-life railroads. People who helped slaves escape and navigate through the wilderness were called conductors; stops along the way were known as stations, overseen by stationmasters; and secret stores of supplies were called depots. Additionally, information about the railroad was often communicated secretly by disguising it as one of the spirituals sung by enslaved blacks. In addition to serving as a mnemonic device, these songs could convey plans to other slaves on how to escape, even while in the presence of slave masters, who would be none the wiser.

overseers. "No day dawns for the slave, nor is it looked for," one slave said. "It is all night—night forever."

Despite slavery's importance to the South's economy, not every Southerner in antebellum America owned slaves. In fact, the overwhelming majority—75 percent—did not, and 88 percent of those that did owned twenty or fewer. It was far more common to see an individual farmer growing just enough to support his family on a small parcel of land, often by himself or with the help of one or two slaves he had purchased, than a huge plantation complex worked by many hundreds of slaves. Nevertheless, the plantation owners came to dominate Southern society, and many small farmers working without slaves still looked up to these wealthy elites in the hopes of someday joining their ranks. As a result, many Southerners saw slave ownership as not only a marker of economic success and social prestige but as a defining cultural institution.

The Growing Storm

For a period of time, the different economic models of the North and the South complemented one another: Northern banks financed the purchase of slaves by Southern plantation owners, who supplied Northern textile mills with cotton grown by slaves. However, the United States underwent several seismic shifts that would pit North and South against one another. This complementary arrangement only worked as long as power on the national level was shared equally between Northern and Southern states.

The Shifting Balance of Power

With the purchase of the Louisiana Territory in 1803, and later the cession of territory in the southwest from Mexico in 1848, the area of the United States was nearly quadrupled. The settlement of these lands raised questions about how they would be incorporated into the Union as states, how they would contribute members to Congress, and how those new representatives and senators would vote. Southern slaveholding states were fearful that any new states in the West would identify as Free States like those in the North. Combined with the North's growing population as a result of the rapid expansion of its industrialized cities and increase in foreign immigration, Southern states feared that the balance of power would shift against them. Should there someday be a vote to abolish slavery throughout the United States, Southern states would be powerless to stop it, threatening the livelihoods of millions of families and disrupting the status quo that had been in place since the beginning of America.

During the early years of the United States, Southerners took political measures to prevent just that situation from happening. During the Constitutional Convention of 1787, the Three-Fifths Compromise ensured that the South's large number of slaves would help to counterbalance the North's growing population. Under the terms of the amendment, each black slave would count as three-fifths of a white person in terms of a state's population, which was used in determining the number of representatives a state contributed to Congress as well as its number of presidential electors. (Ironically, because slaves were

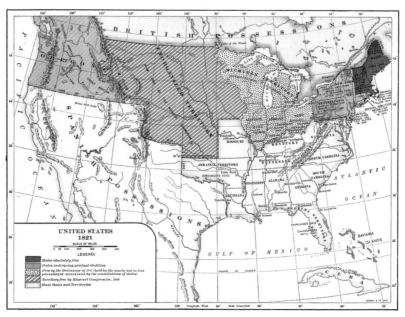

According to the Missouri Compromise, slavery was permitted south of the 36° 30' parallel, as well as throughout Missouri.

considered property, they were denied rights as citizens and therefore did not benefit from this Congressional "representation.")

Later, when Missouri requested permission to join the Union as a slaveholding state in 1819, a fierce debate broke out in the US Congress over whether or not the federal government had the authority to prohibit slavery in states as they entered the Union. As before, a compromise was reached in the interest of preserving the balance of power. Called the Missouri Compromise, the legislation provided a path to allow slaveholding states to be admitted to the Union at the same rate as Free States. Under the terms of the agreement, the status of new states from the Louisiana Territory would be determined by their position in relation to the 36th parallel—those south of the line would be slaveholding, while those north, with the exception of Missouri, would be Free States. In 1820, Missouri joined the Union as a slave state, and Maine (formerly a part of Massachusetts) joined as a Free State.

Violent Politics

The Three-Fifths Compromise and Missouri Compromise attempted to ease tensions over slavery by giving Free States and slave states the latitude to govern themselves within their own territories while ensuring equal representation in the federal government, but America was growing too rapidly for the temporary balance the laws had struck. One catalyst for the increasing unrest centered around one man's fight for freedom. In 1846, a slave named Dred Scott sued for his freedom because his owners had moved from Missouri to the state of Illinois, where slavery was prohibited, and later the Wisconsin Territory, which would have to be organized as a Free State under the Missouri Compromise. Ultimately, the case of *Dred Scott v. Sandford* reached all the way to the Supreme Court. In 1857, the Supreme Court ruled that because Scott was black and the descendant of slaves, he was not a citizen and therefore had no grounds to bring a case to court.

In addition to inflaming passions in both the North and South, the *Dred Scott* decision effectively repealed the Missouri Compromise, erasing the framework that had been designed to maintain the balance of power and peace in the Union. As new territories sought statehood in the 1850s, the principle of "popular sovereignty," in which the voters would determine whether or not a state would allow slavery within its borders, came to replace the Missouri Compromise.

Popular Sovereignty

A famous application of popular sovereignty came with the passage of the Kansas-Nebraska Act of 1854. The act narrowly overcame opposition from Northern politicians, who were outraged that the territories of Kansas and Nebraska, both of which were north of the line established by the Missouri Compromise and therefore should have been admitted as Free States, could potentially become slaveholding territories. As the legislation was voted up, senators on either side of the issue insulted one another and issued death threats. Massachusetts senator and staunch abolitionist Charles Sumner proceeded to give a two-day-long speech on the floor of the Senate called "The Crime Against Kansas," and denounced any policy which allowed slavery to continue.

During the speech, Sumner insulted some of his colleagues, including Senator Andrew Butler of South Carolina. Two days later, South Carolina representative Preston Brooks, a distant cousin of Butler's, approached Sumner in the Senate and proceeded to beat him over the head with a gold-tipped cane, which shattered over the course of the attack. Brooks was charged with assault and fined $300.

As an indicator of the increasingly polarized politics of the time, many newspapers in the South celebrated

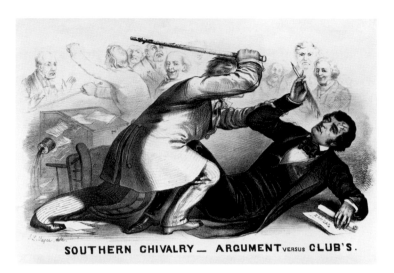

SOUTHERN CHIVALRY — ARGUMENT VERSUS CLUB'S.

Brooks's assault on Sumner was often used by the media to represent the growing tensions between North and South.

the assault. The Richmond, Virginia, newspaper the *Whig* called it "A glorious deed! A most glorious deed!" while others called for yet more outbursts of physical violence. The Richmond *Examiner* wrote, "The abolitionists have been suffered to run too long without collars. They must be lashed into submission." Brooks resigned his office, only to be reelected by his constituents, who also donated canes to replace the one he had broken. As for Sumner, he too was reelected by his home state, but his injuries prevented him from serving, and his seat remained vacant.

The escalating violence that marked the passage of the Kansas-Nebraska Act spilled into the territory.

Thousands of people flooded into the Nebraska Territory in the hopes of swaying the vote one way or another. Disagreements became so heated that violence repeatedly broke out throughout the territory in what was dubbed by the *New York Tribune* as "Bleeding Kansas." Skirmishes between antislavery "Free-Soilers" and the "border ruffians," mostly from Missouri, lasted five years, during which time fifty-six people were killed.

CHAPTER 2

BROTHER AGAINST BROTHER

The issue of slavery in the United States was quickly becoming a vortex of frustration, resentment, and violence engulfing the country from end to end, and all of it would come to a head in the winter of 1860. In November, Abraham Lincoln won the presidency with a landslide electoral victory, beating out the Southern Democrat candidate John Breckenridge by over two-to-one. He had campaigned on a relatively moderate approach to slavery, proposing to allow it in the states where it was already practiced, but to prohibit it in the territories. As an indicator of the country's division, Lincoln

OPPOSITE:
Many of the Civil Wars' important fights took place on the battlefield, but spying played a large role in the outcome of the conflict.

swept the Northern states as well as California and Oregon but did not carry a single Southern one (Lincoln wasn't even listed on the ballot in many Southern states).

In the South, which had already lost its majority in Congress, Lincoln's election was widely seen as the last straw in the North's assault on slavery. Days after the election, the New Orleans *Courier* reported, "The unmistakable fact stares us in the face that we are now in a state of danger unparalleled in the annals of our history … Of one thing, however, the whole South may rest assured—that the sons of Louisiana will not remain indifferent spectators of the drama about to be enacted." A month after the election, the fault lines finally split open. On December 20, in a document whose language closely mirrored that of the Declaration of Independence, the South Carolina legislature formally seceded from the United States. By February 1861, ten more Southern states had followed suit, forming what they called the Confederate States of America. The United States had been split in two.

A Challenging Start

In the years following the American Revolution, military technology and espionage tactics began to lag behind the rest of the world. This was in large part because of America's geographic and political isolation from Europe, which protected it from the frequent, large-scale wars that raged across the continent. Although the United States had dominance in North America, and the possibility of the Civil War had been looming in the background for decades, neither side was prepared by the time it finally arrived. Armies on both sides were small, and even though powerful new firearms such as repeating rifles and pistols were being invented, the soldiers were poorly equipped, relying on outdated weapons. Intelligence gathering, such as the means for collecting, organizing, and analyzing military information, became even more integral to the war effort.

The Confederacy did not have any sort of national organization prior to the Civil War and had to essentially build its government and army from scratch, a large piece of the puzzle when it comes to supporting a network of spies. As difficult as things were for the Confederacy to get its army up to the task of spying, the Union, despite having the power and organization of the federal government behind it, was not in much better shape than their counterparts below the Mason-Dixon Line.

Part of the problem for the Union was understaffing. In December 1860, the same month that South

Carolina seceded, the Federal Army counted just over 16,000 men, well short of the 18,000 troops it was authorized. (By comparison, George Washington fielded approximately 48,000 soldiers at any one time, and a total of 231,000 troops served in the Continental Army during the course of the Revolutionary War.) Understaffing extended beyond the military. When the Southern states started seceding, several politicians resigned their positions and took leadership roles within the Confederacy, leaving vacancies at many of the highest levels of the US government. Chief among such defectors was Jefferson Davis. Appointed US secretary of war in 1853 and elected senator by Mississippi in 1857, Davis resigned on January 21, 1861, when his home state broke with the Union. Davis later went on to become the president of the Confederacy.

Rebels Within the Ranks

The Southern sympathizers who remained often served as moles for the Confederacy. These elected officials and appointees had access to up-to-the-minute developments in Washington, DC, which they then relayed back to their contacts in the South. This sort of penetration is one of the most valuable sources of intelligence for enemy forces in any war, but it usually takes months or years for enemy agents to gain such access, usually at enormous risk and with limited rates of success. In the Civil War, however, the Union was forced to deal with the existence of enemy spies in the government from the very beginning.

In 1861, in an effort to consolidate support for the Union within the federal government, Congress established a committee aimed at identifying Southern spies who retained positions after the start of the war. In a lengthy report issued after hundreds of hearings, the committee found sufficient evidence to identify more than two hundred secessionists within the government. Unfortunately for the Union, the committee had no authority to expel anyone, and only a nominal number of lower-level officials and clerks were terminated.

Battle of Fort Sumter

The problem of widespread disloyalty in the capital played a role in sparking the opening battle of the war. On December 26, 1860, Major Robert Anderson moved the US Army garrison from Fort Moultrie to Fort Sumter, located on an island in the middle of Charleston Harbor. On January 2, 1861, Texas senator Louis T. Wigfall sent a message South Carolina's military, "Holt succeeds Floyd. It means war. Cut

Advance warning from a secessionist agent gave Confederates the advantage during the battle of Fort Sumter.

off supplies from Anderson and take Sumter soon as possible." The South Carolina militia did just that.

A week after Wigfall's message, the Confederates fired on and successfully turned away a federal ship carrying supplies for the garrison. When the South Carolinians intercepted correspondence indicating plans to resupply Anderson, they proceeded to bombard the fort. After three days of shelling, Anderson gave up the fort and with it the last symbol of federal authority in South Carolina.

Surrounded

Complicating the Union's war effort and its sense of security was the location of the nation's capital.

Washington, DC, was bordered by two slave states: Maryland to the north and east and Virginia to the southwest. Ironically, during the formation of the government in the years following the American Revolution, this southerly location of the capital was decided on in 1790 as a concession to the slaveholding states, a symbol of the nation's unity. When Virginia seceded from the Union in April 1861, the only thing separating Washington, DC from the Confederates was the Potomac River. On top of that, Maryland, though it remained with the Union for the duration of the war, was split on the issue of secession. Should Maryland have fallen, the capital would have been completely cut off from the rest of the North, and the center of federal power would have likely fallen into Confederate hands.

DID YOU KNOW?

The only casualties from the Battle of Fort Sumter were suffered after the Union troops had surrendered. As the garrison peacefully evacuated the fort, a cannon primed for a ceremonial salute accidentally exploded, killing one artilleryman and injuring three others, one fatally.

As if the situation was not serious enough, the capital also contained a large number of Confederate sympathizers. One estimate conducted by Charles P. Stone, the commander of the city's militia, counted as many as twenty thousand people—a full third of the population—loyal to the secessionist cause. This included civilians as well as some within the militia itself. In the eyes of one militia captain, the purpose of his unit was to "help keep the Yankees from coming down to coerce the South."

Once Lincoln took office, he ordered seventy-five thousand additional soldiers brought to Washington, DC from throughout the Union, both to begin assembling a proper army as well as to prevent the possibility of any lingering Southern sympathizers from seizing the seat of federal power. Try as it might, however, the Union could not fully erase the existence of Southern spies in the nation's capital.

Spies in the Capital

In April 1861, after Virginia seceded but before it joined the Confederacy, its governor and former congressman John Letcher created a more organized spy network within the capital with access as high as Secretary of State William Seward. Once the war officially began, the Confederacy built on Letcher's spy ring, establishing what became known as the Secret Line. Run by former Baltimore lawyer William Norris and organized under the South's newly created Secret Service Bureau, the Secret Line consisted of a number of couriers who relayed documents and information from Washington, DC, to the eventual capital of the Confederacy, Richmond.

Among the most influential Confederate informants working within Washington, DC, was Rose O'Neal Greenhow. A passionate secessionist and active socialite in Washington society, Greenhow passed information about a Union invasion along the Secret Line. The advanced warning allowed Confederate generals to prepare for the First Battle of Bull Run in July 1861, and ultimately delivered a catastrophic upset to the Federal Army. The prevalence of Southern spies in the Union's capital from the very beginning of the conflict would plague the Union throughout the war, as the flow of information from North to South would continue almost uninterrupted.

Rose O'Neal Greenhow was a Confederate spy.

Pinkerton's Secret Service

Just as the existing structure of the federal government and the abundance of office-holders with ties to the South harmed the Union's ability to keep military secrets, the Confederacy also had spies within its own borders. When the Union first mobilized the Army of the Potomac to defend DC and the surrounding areas, its commander, Major General George B. McClellan, contracted private detectives to fill in the gaps left by the absence of intelligence officers at the start of the Civil War. McClellan contracted the renowned Scottish-born detective Allan Pinkerton, who ran a highly successful private agency in Chicago, Illinois, as his chief intelligence officer.

During the course of his mission to collect information and run counterintelligence operations with the army, Pinkerton organized a large-scale

DID YOU KNOW?

The Pinkerton National Detective Agency hired America's first female detective, Kate Warne, in 1856. Warne convinced Pinkerton that a woman like her could "worm out secrets in many places to which it was impossible for male detectives to gain access."

debriefing program designed to obtain testimony from people crossing over into the North from the South. Although Pinkerton's agents interviewed a variety of people, ranging from Confederate prisoners of war and deserters to businessmen and refugees, Pinkerton realized that the most valuable intelligence to the Union war effort often came from escaped slaves.

Black Dispatches

The intelligence offered by black people was generally trusted by Union soldiers because it was believed they would have no sympathy for the Confederacy. Many were especially motivated to cooperate with the Union in the hopes that truthful testimony would be rewarded with the possibility of freedom. Even after either escaping to the North or being in area relieved by federal troops, black people also helped as soldiers and spies.

The significance of the information from the so-called black dispatches was demonstrated early in the Civil War when the Union was struggling to secure its border. A number of Maryland planters suspected of being a part of a Confederate trafficking ring ferrying military supplies, agents, and military intelligence into Virginia were arrested, but Union troops did not have enough evidence to hold them—until the black servants started talking. One of them,

The Plot to Kill Lincoln

Charles P. Stone, Inspector General of the District of Columbia Militia, was responsible for the safety of President-Elect Lincoln for the innaugural March 1861. Sensing disloyalty within his ranks, Stone hired new detectives. The intelligence these recruits gathered proved invaluable, including, among other secrets, several plots to assassinate Lincoln.

To protect Lincoln, his train route through Baltimore was secretly altered, and a protective detail including detective Allan Pinkerton was put in place. Security at the inauguration was also increased, with a battalion of militia guarding the platform, ranks of

soldiers in front of Lincoln's carriage, and riflemen on the rooftops. Stone maintained, without the intelligence gathered by the detectives, "Mr. Lincoln would never have been inaugurated."

President Lincoln (*center*) is pictured here with Allan Pinkerton (*left*) and Maj. Gen. John A McClernand (*right*).

Thomas Washington, told Union intelligence officials that his master once smuggled two barrels of powder to Confederate contacts in Virginia and quoted him as saying, "I'll assist them all I can, I'll assist 'em ... anything they want as far as I can." Thanks to the testimony of black people such as Washington, the Union could begin restricting the tide of Confederate support flowing from the North to the South.

The Perfect Cover

With slavery enmeshed in Southern culture, black people were in a unique position to obtain information that would otherwise be difficult for a white agent to uncover. The black servants of military officials often accompanied their masters to extremely high-level war meetings, where they were exposed to firsthand information about troop strength, strategies, and more. These agents-in-place could operate undetected within enemy territory and funnel details back to the Union.

Slavery also provided a cover for Union scouts, who could pose as laborers around Confederate fortifications and infiltrate without raising suspicion, and the intellect of black servants was largely overlooked due to Southern prejudices. Taken together, these qualities made blacks the perfect spies, and the Union took full advantage of it where they could.

The capacity of blacks to serve as spies was so great that in 1863, the Confederate general Robert E. Lee identified them as "the chief source of information to the enemy." Ironically, because slavery was one of the Confederacy's most important cultural institutions, it was also its greatest liability.

One of the Union's most famous spies was Harriet Tubman, but despite running one of the most successful spy rings, she is rarely remembered for her contributions to the war effort at all. Most people remember Harriet Tubman for her work in the Underground Railroad, especially as a conductor, communicating information to enslaved people and leading them away from their owners, which was one of the most vulnerable and dangerous parts of the route. These connections made her an incredible asset to the Union war effort because she was already familiar with the secret paths into and out of the South and had a network of abolitionist sympathizers who could funnel information to her.

Harriet Tubman was part of a network of antislavery activists and a spy for the North during the Civil War.

When she died in 1913, she was buried with military honors in gratitude for her service.

Unfortunately, despite the importance of black people to the Union's war effort, the stories and identities of most black spies have been lost to history. In the years following the Civil War, the racial prejudice against blacks, which remained common in both the North and South, meant that the contributions of black people to the war were disregarded and largely forgotten. Black agents still living in the South may have even been motivated to erase their accomplishments themselves, out of fear for their own lives or those of their families should word of their activities have gotten out. Despite the void of information, the contributions of black people to the Civil War is to be commemorated, as Frederick Douglass wrote: "The true history of this war will show that the loyal army found no friends at the South so faithful, active, and daring in their efforts to sustain the government as the Negroes."

CHAPTER 3

CIVIL WAR
SPY TECH

A t the outbreak of the Civil War, both the Union and the Confederacy were forced to develop strategies to address the need to collect and analyze information. Neither side organized a formal central intelligence agency; instead, individual generals relied on the reconnaissance units that they themselves had organized. Typically called Secret Service, these units were comprised of cavalry scouts, who provided battlefield details such as enemy troop movements and numbers, and private detectives, who collected communications

OPPOSITE:
Union semaphore officers sent coded messages using flags to communicate with stations across the battlefield.

such as intercepted letters and telegrams as well as testimony from captured prisoners, defectors, and private citizens.

At the same time that the Union and Confederate generals were building their intelligence networks, several exciting new technologies were being developed that would usher in a new modern era, and the armies raced to bring these new inventions to the battlefield.

Communication

Of the many problems an army faces during a campaign, one of the trickiest is how to maintain clear and efficient lines of communication. On the one hand, soldiers and officers needed to report information like troop progress, positioning, battle outcomes, and so on to their superiors; on the other, those decision-makers then had to use that information to issue orders back through the chain of command.

The Signal Corps

During the Civil War, the generals on both sides had several factors to consider when it came to military communication channels. The first of these was the large distances that often existed between troops and their commanding officers. In order to transmit

Some semaphore signalmen would intercept and interpret enemy signals by using raised towers and telescopes.

messages across these distances, both armies made use of the semaphore system. A semaphore is a visual messaging system in which flags are held in certain arrangements to signify letters. To the untrained eye, semaphore seems like random waving of flags, leading to the nickname "wig wag."

Working from a hilltop or other raised platform, soldiers trained as semaphore signalmen could communicate with one another from opposite ends of a battlefield. At night, signalmen could also use torches instead of flags. Both sides of the Civil War had dedicated Signal Corps, and the connection between battlefield signaling and spying was so strong that the South's Secret Service Bureau was actually formed as a subgroup within the Confederate Signal Corps.

Technology Tackling Distance and Time

The faster information could be relayed back and forth across distances, the faster the armies could act. The semaphore system excelled at relaying brief messages across short distances but was not a practical solution for communications between battlefield officers and commanders working out of the capital. Bad weather could interrupt the line of sight between signalmen, and an enemy ambush on just one station would disrupt the entire chain. In the period of weeks it took a rider traverse the wilderness to pass messages, the initial situation might have changed. What if instead of traveling at the speed of horse, messages could travel faster—as fast as the speed of light? At the beginning of the Civil War, one particular invention promised to achieve just that.

The Telegraph

In the 1830s two British inventors named Sir William Cooke and Sir Charles Wheatstone applied the scientific advancements made over the early nineteenth century to invent the world's first practical electrical telegraph. The word telegraph comes from the Greek word *tele*, meaning "at a distance," and *graphein*, which means "to write." The device was comprised of a series of needles that rotated around a diamond-shaped board, called a dial, which was marked with numbers and letters. As an operator on one end manipulated his dial, electric current traveled through a series of wires, and the electromagnetic current they produced manipulated two needles on the dial on the other end, which together pointed to a specific letter on the dial. Cooke and Wheastone's telegraph was soon implemented in England's railway system and helped to standardize times and schedules across the country.

At the same time that Cooke and Wheatstone were developing their telegraph, an American painter named Samuel Morse became interested in electromagnetic principles while on a cruise ship returning from Europe. When he got back to the United States, Morse began work on his own electric telegraph, developing a special code—Morse code—to be used with his telegraph. Morse's design required an operator who would depress a battery-connected pointer and complete the electric circuit. Based on the length of the depression, a dot (short) or a dash (long) signal is sent across a wire and manipulates an electromagnetic stylus on the receiving end, which in turn makes indentations on a paper tape that could then be translated into their corresponding letters and numbers.

Although Morse's telegraph system relied on a specialized code instead of indicating specific alphanumeric symbols, the biggest advantage his design had over Cooke and Wheatstone's was its simplicity. Morse's telegraph only required one wire to complete its circuit, as opposed to the several in Cooke and Wheatstone's. In addition to reducing cost and improving ease of operation, the single-wire design meant that an electric signal, which tends to become weaker over distance, could travel farther before degrading and was more easily boosted to cross even greater distances.

In 1843, Samuel Morse won a $30,000 grant from Congress in order to construct an experimental long-distance telegraph line, but support for his plan was far from unanimous. Many considered Morse's idea ludicrous, and the vote passed narrowly, with just six votes more in favor and seventy congressmen abstaining. Nevertheless, a year later, Morse successfully completed the first test of the line. Operating from Baltimore, Maryland, the message sped across 40 miles (64 km) of copper wire suspended by trees and poles to Washington, DC. An instant later, a receiver in the Supreme Court translated Morse's message: "What hath God wrought."

Over the next ten years, 23,000 miles (37,000 km) of telegraph lines would be constructed throughout the United States. The earliest adopters were newspapers,

President Lincoln's relationship with the telegraph changed
when an office opened in the War Department building in 1862.

banks, and railroads, who recognized the potential of
the new technology. The US government lagged far
behind, and before 1862, President Lincoln had only
sent approximately one telegram per month. Everything
changed in May of that year, when a telegraph office
opened up in the War Department building, located
next to the White House. Lincoln sent nine telegrams
May 24, and sent more in the following week than he
had over the course of his presidency.

The appeal of instant communication caused
Lincoln to visit the telegraph office several times a day,
and occasionally even sleep there to be woken with up-

to-the-minute reports from the battlefield. He would collect and read through copies of all the telegrams the office received, regardless of whether they were meant for him or not. Thanks to the telegraph, Lincoln could receive direct reports from and issue commands to his generals in the field—as well as keep an ear tuned to the chatter sent around Washington, DC.

Reading Between (and Behind) the Lines

Although both the semaphore system and the electric telegraph operated on a fundamental level using codes, both forms of communication were vulnerable to interception and deception. A scout need only find a line of sight to an enemy signal tower in order to read messages, and permanent observation towers and hilltop telescope placements could prevent signalmen from sending messages altogether. Telegraph lines could be wiretapped, though actual cases were rare, and messages transmitted via telegraph that had been written down could be found or stolen. Invading soldiers could seize control of an enemy telegraph office before the operator could report the news and begin posing as friendly forces. How could Civil War commanders communicate without having their messages captured and read by the enemy? The trick was to write the messages in a way that they were unreadable by anyone other than the intended recipient—the trick was cryptography.

Hiding Information

Cryptography, the science of writing in codes, has a long and interesting history stretching back almost as far as language itself. By the time of the Civil War, cryptographers had devised dozens of ways to encode sensitive messages, and many of these were in use throughout the course of the war, ranging from the simple to the complex and even unbreakable. In some cases, when time was of the essence or a more complex code could not be agreed on, telegraph operators relied on simple and sometimes even silly codes, such as this coded message, originally ordered by President Lincoln to be sent to Major General Ambrose Burnside:

> Can Inn Ale me withe 2 oak out Ann pas Ann me flesh ends N. V. Corn Inn out with U cud Inn heaven day nest Wed roe Moore Tom darkey hat Greek Why Hawk of Abbott Inn B chewed I if.

The message is written backwards and uses a simple encryption method known as phonetic substitution.

Successful interception of the messages speeding across the thousands of miles of telegraph lines could potentially sway the outcome of a battle, a campaign, or even the war itself. Although the volume of information made the telegraph a tantalizing target for wiretapping, it was easier to simply destroy the lines, and therefore only a handful of cases were recorded during the Civil War. In his journal, David Homer Bates, manager of the Union War Department's telegraph office, wrote of one such instance.

During the 1862 Fredericksburg campaign, Union telegraph operators noticed circuits were opening and closing in a way that they did not recognize, leaving a phantom telegraphic signature. Suspecting a Confederate had wiretapped the line, they began transmitting fake information, and a troop of linemen was dispatched along the length of the wire.

The Confederate operator, for his part, recognized he had been caught, and sent "in reply a lot of balderdash." Ultimately he transmitted that he was from General Robert E. Lee's army and had been listening in on the federls for several days. Bates and his colleagues "gossiped with him for a while" before the signal disappeared. When Union scouts located the remains of the hacker's camp, they discovered he had skillfully made the connection using a fine silk-covered wire that blended nearly seamlessly with the line.

Reading the message aloud slowly from the end to the beginning reveals the hidden information (here's a tip: the word "flesh" also means "meat"):

If I should be in boat off Aquia Creek at dark tomorrow (Wednesday) evening, could you, without inconvenience, meet me and pass an hour or two with me?

In order to protect the whereabouts of President Lincoln, the message needed to be encrypted, but due to time constraints (the meeting was going to take place the next day), telegraph operators did not have time to set up and agree on a stronger code with their colleagues in Virginia. So even though this was a relatively simple code that may easily be cracked should it fall into enemy hands, the message was sent. Fortunately, the Confederates were unable to translate the message.

A more complex code that was in frequent use throughout the course of the Civil War, especially by the Confederacy, was the polyalphabetic cipher. A polyalphabetic cipher works by starting with a keyword (or words), which is written above the message that is being encrypted. Each letter of the message corresponds with a letter in the keyword above, which is repeated as many times for the length of the message. Using a tool called an alphabet square, the cryptographer finds a third letter that corresponds with both the letter in the keyword and the letter in the original message. The letters in this new message are then written down, forming the encrypted message. In order to decode the message, the recipient, who is provided with the secret keyword, refers to a copy of the chart that the cryptographer used and cross-references it with the letters in the encrypted message to reveal the original message.

Deciphering Tool

In composing messages protected by the polyalphabetic cipher, the Confederates also used a cipher disk. This device consisted of two circular platters, one stationary and a smaller one on top of it that rotated, each with characters written around the perimeter. As the movable disk rotated around the board, the symbols on it aligned with those on the fixed disk, creating a new alphabet square with each use. This added an extra layer of complexity, and therefore security and secrecy, to the polyalphabetic cipher. Confederate spies using the same cipher disk design with an agreed-upon alignment of the letters could still easily decode each other's messages, but Union troops that captured a cipher disk could not because they could not rely on the arrangement of the symbols to be accurate.

The cipher disk allowed Confederate spies to carry a revisable alphabet chart everywhere they went.

The Union also had its own version of the cipher disk, the federal cipher, but this one was used by the Signal Corps to change the meaning of visual signals. Unlike the Confederate polyalphabetic cipher, the federal cipher disk only changed the symbol for a particular letter without the added complexity of translating a message through a code word.

The US Military Telegraph Corps

The telegraph was among the most important tools at the Union's disposal. Lincoln's reliance on the telegraph eventually lead to the formation of the US Military Telegraph Corps, a division of the War Department. Its head, Anson Stager, was among the most brilliant cryptographers of all time. Among his contributions to the war effort was a code, named the Stager Cipher, which proved so complicated that the Confederacy never succeeded in cracking it.

The corps was tasked with not only transmitting and receiving messages to and from the battlefield but also devising codes and cracking Confederate ones. Among them was a message, recounted by Union telegraph operator David Homer Bates, which was given to him by Major General Ulysses S. Grant during the Confederate siege of Vicksburg, Virginia:

Lieutenant General Pemberton: My X A F V. U S L X was V V U F L S J P by the B R C Y A (I) J 200 000 V E G T. S U A J. N E R P. Z I F M. It will be G F O E C S Z O (Q) D as they N T Y M N X. Bragg M J T P H I

N Z G a Q R (K) C M K B S E. When it D
Z G J X. I will Y O I G. AS. Q H Y. N I T
W M do you Y T I A M the I I K M. V F V
E Y. How and where is the J S Q M L G U
G S F T V E. H B F Y is your R O E E L.

J. E. Johnston

Although some of the message is recognizable,
the most important words have been encrypted and
therefore look like nonsense. Without the keyword,
the Union codebreakers were forced to resort to trial
by error, guessing at the words as they went. Bates later
learned that the key was in fact "MANCHESTER
BLUFF," but even without it, he and his associates
were able to decode the message, which read:

Lieutenant-General Pemberton, Vicksburg:
My—— was captured by the picket.
200,000 caps have been sent. It will be
increased as they arrive. Bragg is sending a
division. When it joins I will come to you.
What do you think the best route? How
and where is the enemy operating? What is
your force?

J. E. Johnston

The World's First Modern War

In addition to the exciting new advancements in electronic communication, the Civil War era also saw improvements in transportation technologies at land, sea, and even in the air. The invention of the steam engine at the turn of the seventeenth century eventually led to the railroad and steamships, both of which made the Civil War what could be considered the world's first modern war. The railroad allowed armies to mobilize faster and made it easier to keep forces supplied. Many historians have said that the Union's more advanced railroad technology and larger network of rails was one of the biggest reasons why the North eventually won the war. The steam-powered naval ship, meanwhile, was truly a force to be reckoned with during sea-based and joint land-and-sea operations. Unlike contemporary "tall ships" powered by sails, steamships could move in any direction and could sit lower in the water, which protected them from artillery fire from forts and other vessels. Both the North and the South eventually improved on the steamship by adding thick iron and steel plating, which deflected all but the most powerful artillery blasts, leading to the development of so-called ironclad-class warships.

Spying from Above

Perhaps the most groundbreaking innovation had nothing to do with the ground at all. The turn of the nineteenth century saw the development of lighter-than-air gas-filled balloons that were capable of holding passengers and equipment. Before the Civil War, balloons were generally considered to be a novelty enjoyed by eccentric scientists and fairgoers, but the Federal Army was still curious about the reconnaissance potential of balloons. The success of the world's first balloon reconnaissance mission, at the 1794 Battle of Fleurus during the French Revolutionary Wars, was debated, and the French Aerostatic Corps was eventually disbanded. The Union's first military balloon, used at First Bull Run, was accidentally destroyed.

In the summer of 1861, an Ohio balloonist named Thaddeus S. C. Lowe, undeterred by the early failures of aerial reconnaissance, made a bold demonstration of the balloon's military capability. On June 16, 1861, Lowe ascended in his personal balloon, the *Enterprise*, rising 500 feet (152 meters) above the National Mall in Washington, DC. Using a telegraph key attached to a wire wound around the cable that tethered him to the ground, Lowe delivered a message personally addressed to Abraham Lincoln. The president was impressed, and he authorized Lowe to head up the Union Army

The *Intrepid* was used to collect intelligence during the Battle of Seven Pines.

Balloon Corps, comprised of civilian operators, and gave him the funds to build eight military balloons capable of reaching heights up to 5,000 feet (1,524 m).

This blending of aerial observation and electrical communication was put to the test later that summer. On September 24, Lowe rose to the skies above Arlington, Virginia, in the newly built *Union* and began telegraphing information about the position of Confederate troops approximately 3 miles (4.8 km) away. Working off Lowe's intelligence, a Union artillery battery without a clear line of sight to the Confederate encampment began firing and accurately hit their targets. The balloons could make observations of enemy forces that were still a day's march away or further, and became one of the most important lines of defense securing Washington, DC, from Confederate forces who could mobilize just on the other side of the Potomac.

The Union army employed aeronauts like Lowe throughout the Civil War. Although Lowe's initial demonstration was based on communicating via telegraph, the technology could sometimes be finicky, and the fragile electrical wires wrapped around tether cables occasionally snapped. As a work-around, aeronauts were trained in the semaphore system of flag signals to communicate with the ground. Lowe himself sometimes even made handwritten notes, drawings, and maps, which he placed in canisters and zipped down the tether to assistants. The Union balloonists proved so effective that the Confederacy tried to create its own aerial reconnaissance unit, but lack of money, mismanagement, and battlefield confusion doomed the project. Although the Union balloonists provided valuable intelligence and even changed the way future wars would be fought, the civilians who made up the Balloon Corps struggled to find respect among the military. Ballooning could not shake its reputation as the realm of mad scientists and carnival sideshows, and the project was eventually canceled.

One espionage tactic used throughout history has been to weaken an enemy by inflating, or devaluing, currency. All governments carefully control the amount of money that they put into circulation: print too little, and goods are too expensive for people to afford; print too much, and the money people have becomes worthless. If a spy organization can successfully mimic the money of an enemy government and flood the country with counterfeit, or fake, bills, they can actually cause serious economic problems for the other side. Oddly enough, the most successful counterfeiting operation of the Civil War happened unintentionally.

Between March 1862 and August 1863, Samuel Upham, a general store owner in Philadelphia, printied $15 million in high-quality copies of a Confederate five-dollar bill. Upham called the fakes "mementos of the Rebellion," which he sold as souvenirs of what was at first considered a brief rebel uprising. Upham

The only thing identifying Upham's reproductions was a small removable tab that read "Fac-simile [replica] Confederate Note."

wasn't technically in the counterfeiting business because at the bottom of every note he included a tab with the words "Fac-simile [replica] Confederate Note" along with his name and address. However, with the tabs removed, the notes were indistinguishable from the genuine articles issued by the Confederate government.

Upham's fakes were so popular that his store frequently sold out, and Union troops used the copies to pay for everything from supplies to accommodations and horses throughout the South. The value of the Confederate dollar dropped 90 percent, causing distrust and sparking riots.

The Confederacy claimed the fakes were part of a deliberate Union conspiracy to undermine the government and accused its mastermind of "Yankee scoundrelism." The Confederate Congress made counterfeiting a capital crime punishable by death and attached a $10,000 bounty to a warrant for Upham's arrest.

Although never officially licensed by the Union, Upham was also never ordered to stop because the Union did not recognize Confederate money as legitimate currency to begin with. Upham's business caused incalculable harm to the Confederate government.

CHAPTER 4

THE LEGACY OF CIVIL WAR SPYING

E ven without centralized intelligence agencies, the Civil War was directly impacted by the activities of covert agents and their communications. Though there is disagreement among historians about the turning point to the war, many claim it was the Union victory at the Battle of Gettysburg, and while it is true the battle on July 1–3, 1863, was the bloodiest and most infamous fight of the war, the end was the result of a string of events, and espionage played a role in the outcome.

After the Union capture of New Orleans in April 1862, the Confederacy lost both its greatest port and support abroad. Under Major General Benjamin

OPPOSITE:
Confederate general Robert E. Lee
surrenders to Union commander
Ulysses S. Grant at the Battle of
Appomattox Court House.

Butler, the city was held under strict occupation. What's more, Butler built a base of support among the poor classes, and he created a wide-ranging intelligence and counterintelligence network.

The South's defeat at Gettysburg can also be credited in part to intelligence activity, or rather the lack thereof. Robert E. Lee's strategy was flawed from the very beginning because J. E. B. Stuart, the "eyes of the army," failed to provide accurate information regarding Union troop movements.

Following the fall of Atlanta in September 1864, the Union controlled the transportation hub and most fortified city of the South. This victory bolstered Union support of Lincoln just in time for his reelection. Union troops continued to win victories on the battlefields. On April 9, 1865, Robert E. Lee surrendered to the Army of the Potomac, although Confederate forces continued to fight for several months. On August 20, 1866, President Andrew Johnson was finally able to sign Proclamation 157: "Declaring that Peace, Order, Tranquillity, and Civil Authority Now Exists in and Throughout the Whole of the United States of America."

The technology and tactics used by Civil War spies had lasting impacts on American and even global society for years to come. Information proved to be a valuable tool and powerful weapon. What had

Reigniting the Civil War

On the night of April 14, 1865, at Ford's Theatre in Washington, DC, actor John Wilkes Booth approached Lincoln, drew a pistol, and shot him point-blank in the head before leaping from the balcony and escaping the city on horseback.

The assassination, which took place just days after General Robert E. Lee surrendered the last major Confederate army at Appomattox Court House, Virginia, was part of a Confederate conspiracy to reignite the Civil War. At the same time as Booth's attack, another man named Lewis Powell attempted to kill Secretary of State William Seward in his home (Seward survived). Just as Union intelligence failed to uncover the plot and stop Booth, the South also failed in the attempt to prolong the war.

While the nation mourned Lincoln, the largest manhunt in United States history got underway, led by the army intelligence officer Lafayette C. Baker. After a thirteen-day chase, Union cavalry surrounded the barn on a Virginia tobacco farm where Booth and another conspirator had been hiding; during their capture, Booth was shot and died just hours later.

John Wilkes Booth shoots President Lincoln at Ford's Theatre, Washington, DC.

started as a neglected, almost nonexistent, part of American government, intelligence organizations in the United States experienced improved development and organization, ultimately leading to the high-tech, centralized government-run agencies we know today, such as the Federal Bureau of Investigation (FBI) and the Central Intelligence Agency (CIA). Even the Secret Service, once a general term for whatever activities and individuals were employed in the course of collecting and analyzing military intelligence, became the name for a formal organization devoted to investigating cases of currency counterfeiting and later to protecting the president and his family.

Modern Warfare in the Skies

The communication and transportation technologies of the Civil War became the precursors of even more advancements in the next decades. Although the federal government had eventually scrapped balloon reconnaissance by the end of the war, aerial observation became an important part of future wars. The turn of the twentieth century saw the invention of the fixed-wing, self-propelled aircraft, designed by Ohio-based bicycle mechanics Orville and Wilbur Wright. Long thought impossibile, the heavier-than-air airplane

The Civil War-era balloon barge *George Washington Park Custis* paved the way for today's modern aircraft carriers.

allowed for sustained flights in any direction and up to far greater distances than the Civil War balloonists could ever imagine.

The airplane became an important part of both conventional warfare as well as spying: during the Cold War, which was fought between the United States and the Soviet Union in the decades following World War II, specially designed U-2 spy planes took photographs of enemy nuclear missile installations and other military targets from altitudes of up to

Like Civil War balloons, unarmed U-2 spy planes gathered aerial reconnaissance of military sites during the Cold War.

70,000 feet (21,336 m). Today, unmanned aerial reconnaissance aircraft such as Predator drones have become an important piece in the war on terror. Operated by airmen half a world away, drones are used to observe enemy positions and movements and even fire laser-guided "bunker busting" missiles.

Communication Technology

The most important development to both the military and society as a whole had been in the realm of electrical communication and encryption. Samuel Morse's telegraph came to be an indispensable part of American life in the years following the Civil War, becoming an important tool for the government, businesses, and private citizens to keep in touch with one another and communicate the day's information across an expanding country.

A decade after the Civil War, the US government granted a patent to the scientist and inventor Alexander Graham Bell for an incredible new device: the telephone. Using the principles of electromagnetism and electric force, Bell's device allowed people to communicate directly with one another in their own voices, without the use of specially trained operators translating the dots and dashes that came from the other side. Although the telegraph continued to be an important communication technology well into the twentieth century, it was eventually replaced by the telephone.

The Computer

The legacy of Morse's telegraph did not stop there, though. The twentieth century saw the invention of the computer, a new kind of device that would again

DID YOU KNOW?

During the course of the war, President Lincoln insisted that the federal flag include the full number of stars representing all the states in the Union, including those that had seceded.

completely change the course of history. The first computers were mechanical devices that ran off of the electric grid, using electromagnetic impulses to drive numerical calculations. Although many people mistakenly draw a line between advanced digital devices, like computers, with simpler mechanical ones, like, say, a toaster, the term "digital" actually refers to the language of those devices, which is numerical.

This language used by new computers can also trace its roots back to Morse's telegraph. Morse's improvement on Cooke and Wheatstone's telegraph, which communicated using alphanumeric symbols, was the distinct dots and dashes that simplified the transmission and could later be translated into regular

Computers communicate in a language known as binary, which isn't much different from Morse's telegraph code.

One of the more controversial legacies of the Civil War is the practice of government surveillance, or spying on citizens. Abraham Lincoln's habit of reading all telegrams passing through the War Department, regardless if they were addressed to him or not, proved beneficial from a national security standpoint. The interceptions yielded valuable intelligence that prevented some of the most catastrophic plots, including a plan to set fire to New York City, from becoming realized; however, these early instances of government surveillance amounted to a serious breach in privacy for citizens.

Although there is no specific right to privacy in the Constitution of the United States, it has long been argued that there is an implied expectation the government will keep out of the personal business of citizens. The debate between protecting the privacy of the people and protecting the nation's security has not been settled even today. Over the course of the war on terror, initiated by President George W. Bush in the wake of the terrorist attacks on September 11, 2001, whistleblowers have revealed that the government has engaged in large-scale spying on citizens. Government organizations such as the National Security Agency (NSA) routinely collect data about practically every individual within and without the United States.

alphanumeric symbols. It was the same with computers once they were invented, but instead of dots and dashes, they communicate through zeros and ones—binary—a language that simplifies human language and allows the machines to perform incredibly fast calculations and processes, faster even than humans themselves.

It may seem surprising at first glance to imagine Morse's simple telegraph leading up to today's most powerful computers and smartphones, but the telegraph paved the way for digital devices in important ways. The telegraph cables that crisscrossed the country eventually gave way to the telephone lines, and in the process developed an important infrastructure that would be used to connect virtually every American to DSL internet in the 1990s.

1797 Delegates at a Constitutional Convention agree on the Three-Fifths Compromise for accounting for slaves in representation and electoral vote calculations.

circa 1800s A secret network to shuttle southern slaves to freedom is formed; eventually becoming the Underground Railroad.

1800 Lighter-than-air balloons invented.

1820 Missouri and Maine enter the Union as slaveholding and Free States, respectively. Congress agrees on the Missouri Compromise for determining the issue of slavery in the Western territories.

1844 Samuel Morse successfully transmits telegraph message from Baltimore, Maryland, to Washington, DC.

1857 The Supreme Court decision on *Dred Scott v. Sanford* declares the Missouri Compromise unconstitutional.

1854 Kansas-Nebraska Act passes Congress.

1860 Republican Abraham Lincoln is elected president of the United States. South Carolina becomes the first state to secede from the Union on December 20.

Jan. 1861 President Lincoln is secretly ferried through Baltimore, Maryland, in the dead of night by private detective Allan Pinkerton to avoid a secessionist assassination plot.

**April
1861**   Virginia governor John Letcher organizes the Secret Line, an intelligence network tunneling information from Washington, DC, to Richmond, Virginia.

**July
1861**   Confederate forces, given advance information by Washington-based spy Rose O'Neal Greenhow, successfully defeat a Union army at Bull Run.

**June
1861**   Thaddeus Lowe performs test of aerial reconnaissance balloon above the National Mall in Washington, DC.

**Sept.
1861**   Thaddeus Lowe aboard the military balloon Union observes the position of Confederate forces near Arlington, Virginia, to a federal battery. The bombardment is the first use of aerial observation in indirect artillery fire.

**May
1862**   A telegraph office opens up in the War Department adjacent to the White House; visits to the office to send telegraphs and read all incoming messages becomes part of President Lincoln's daily routine.

**April
1865**   General Robert E. Lee surrenders the last major Confederate army to General Ulysses S. Grant at Appomattox Court House, Virginia. John Wilkes Booth assassinates President Lincoln at Ford's Theatre in Washington, DC, and is fatally wounded during capture.

Glossary

abolitionist A person in favor of ending slavery within the United States.

antebellum The period of time before a war, especially the Civil War.

cipher A way of writing that disguises the meaning.

code A system of symbols used to communicate secretly.

cryptography The study of writing and solving encoded messages.

detective A person whose job is to investigate; during the Civil War, private detectives were contracted by the Union and Confederate governments to collect military intelligence.

industrialized Characterized by the growth of manufacturing and business.

informant Someone who provides information, usually of a sensitive nature, to another.

intelligence Information that is of a military value.

mole A spy who works from within an enemy organization, such as government, usually holding a high position.

popular sovereignty The principle that citizens should determine the laws by which they are governed; before the Civil War, popular sovereignty allowed citizens in new territories to determine whether or not slavery would be allowed in their area.

reconnaissance Strategic military observation of a location.

secede To formally withdraw from an organization or government.

semaphore A visual system of communication, such as through flags or light signals.

telegraph (electric) A communication system in which messages are transmitted over a wire using electromagnetic impulses.

Further Information

Books

Abbott, Karen. *Liar, Temptress, Soldier, Spy: Four Women Undercover in the Civil War.* New York: HarperCollins, 2014.

Allen, Thomas B. *Harriet Tubman, Secret Agent: How Daring Slaves and Free Blacks Spied for the Union During the Civil War.* Washington, DC: National Geographic, 2006.

Fishel, Edwin C. *The Secret War for the Union: The Untold Story of Military Intelligence in the Civil War.* New York: Houghton Mifflin, 1996

Swanson, James L. *Manhunt: The 12-Day Chase for Lincoln's Killer.* New York: William Morrow, 2006.

Websites

Atlas Obscura: Inside the Manhunt for John Wilkes Booth

www.atlasobscura.com/articles/the-manhunt-for-john-wilkes-booth

This article from Atlas Obscura offers a summary of the assassination of Lincoln, a day-by-day breakdown of the events following, photographs, and an interactive map of the route the conspirators took in their escape.

Central Intelligence Agency: Black Dispatches: Black American Contributions to Union Intelligence During the Civil War

www.cia.gov/library/center-for-the-study -of-intelligence/csi-publications/books-and -monographs/black-dispatches/index.html

This article celebrates the incredible achievements of black Americans by exploring a handful of black spies's most harrowing stories.

Civil War Trust: Civil War Ballooning During the Seven Days Campaign

www.civilwar.org/learn/articles/civil-war -ballooning-during-seven-days-campaign

A detailed look at the history and uses of balloons in aerial reconnaissance during the Civil War, including photographs and color illustrations.

US Naval Landing Party: Secret Codes in the Civil War

www.usnlp.org/games/coding.pdf

The naval warfare enthusiasts at the US Naval Landing Party provide this printable document on Civil War codes. In addition to an explainer of how polyalphabetic ciphers work, this site also features a template to make your own working cipher disk!

Bates, David Homer. *Lincoln in the Telegraph Office: Recollections of the United States Military Telegraph Corps During the Civil War.* New York: The Century Co., 1907.

Fishel, Edwin C. *The Secret War for the Union: The Untold Story of Military Intelligence in the Civil War.* New York: Houghton Mifflin, 1996.

"George Washington, Spymaster." Mount Vernon. org. Accessed September 24, 2017. http://www. mountvernon.org/george-washington/the-revolutionary-war/spying-and-espionage/george-washington-spymaster/.

Kiger, Patrick. "Lincoln's Codebreakers." WETA.org. November 19, 2013. Accessed September 24, 2017. https://blogs.weta.org/boundarystones/2013/11/19/lincolns-codebreakers.

"Polyalphabetic Substitution Ciphers" Cornell.edu. March 18, 2004. Accessed September 24, 2017. https://www.math.cornell.edu/~mec/2003-2004/cryptography/polyalpha/polyalpha.html.

Rose, P. K. "Black Dispatches: Black American Contributions to Union Intelligence During the Civil War." Central Intelligence Agency.gov. July 07, 2008. Accessed September 24, 2017. https://www.cia.gov/library/center-for-the-study-of-intelligence/csi-publications/books-and-monographs/black-dispatches/index.html.

Van Doren Stern, Philip. *Secret Missions of the Civil War.* New Jersey: Wings Books, 1990.

Wheeler, Tom. "The First Wired President." New York Times. May 24, 2012. Accessed September 24, 2017. https://opinionator.blogs.nytimes.com/2012/05/24/the-first-wired-president/?mcubz=3.

Index

Andrew Coddington is a freelance writer and editor who has written a number of books on history and politics, including *Mass Government Surveillance: Spying on Citizens* in Cavendish Square Publishing's Spying, Surveillance, and Privacy in the 21st Century series. He is also the author of *Code Breakers and Spies of the Vietnam War*. He lives in Buffalo, New York, with his wife and dog.